Sketching
Basics

A.FAERY

Alois Fabry.

Sketching Basics

ALOIS FABRY

Mud Puddle Books
NEW YORK

Sketching Basics
By Alois Fabry

© 1958 by The Viking Press, Inc.
© Renewed 1986 by Sally Sawyer Fabry

This edition published in 2010 by
Mud Puddle Books, Inc.
54 W. 21st Street
Suite 601
New York, NY 10010
info@mudpuddlebooks.com

ISBN: 978-1-60311-033-4

Originally published as
Sketching is Fun with Pen & Pencil by
The Viking Press, Inc.
New York

Printed and bound in China

Contents

Introduction

THE URGE TO EXPRESS ONESELF finds a natural outlet in drawing. Since childhood we have all been using pencils and pens, and whether we realize it or not, we have, in a certain sense, been drawing all the time with these mediums. We use pencils and pens more than any other tools in our daily rounds: we write letters with them, scribble, make out checks, write out shopping lists, send notes, make notations, draw diagrams and directions, and doodle. Pencils and pens are, in fact, our closest companions, yet how much do we really know about them? Concentrating on pencils, this book will show the variety of pencils available and the effects possible by using them in different ways.

Ever since time began, drawing has been used as a direct means of communication. Prehistoric man wished to record the triumphal hunt, so he drew his experiences in a direct, expressive manner on the walls of caves. Many artists today have been influenced by the works of the primitives and they render nature

Rock Painting, Niaux Cave, France.

boldly and in its simplest terms. But there are many different ways of drawing. We can choose to be primitively modern; equally we can draw inspiration from the classical works of the past. There is an abundance of illustrated material to guide us in whichever path we wish to follow.

Drawings serve a number of purposes—they may be mere doodlings or more studied sketches for future use. They may be realistic or merely suggestive. They may express a mood or movement, a delightful scene, a detail, a character, or caricature. Drawings can be strong and powerful or light and gay, depending on the character and mood of the artist. The mere stroke of a pencil can express movement or stillness, anger or tenderness, sorrow or humor. Like handwriting, drawing expresses character and should remain as individual as possible.

Before the advent of oil painting, drawing was an entire art in itself; the cave drawings, hieroglyphs, and medieval books show this. Later, drawings also became a preliminary step in a painting. During the Renaissance, artists made hundreds of preliminary drawings and sketches, of drapery folds, figures in action, heads, hands, and other details that needed careful study before painting the finished work. There were, however, artists who continued to do drawings purely for the sake of drawing, such as Michelangelo, Dürer, Holbein, Daumier, and Rowlandson. There are artists and illustrators who do it today.

Many of our great modern artists—Picasso, for instance, and Matisse—have done pen drawings for the sheer joy of working in this graphic medium. For these artists, the line becomes a living thing, an expressive idiom which retains a freshness of approach not always attainable in paintings.

Drawing, whether in pen or pencil, is not only essential for any work of art, but is the basis for all good art. Artists can draw

Alfred Sisley. "River Loing."

and live by selling their drawings, or they can paint. But before painting they must know how to draw.

The projects in this book are based on the course I have been giving for years, and many of the illustrations used are the work of young students who have had no lessons other than those given in the following pages.

Alois Fabry

Henri Matisse. "Portrait of a Lady."

Albrecht Dürer. Sketch. Young Girl.

PROJECT **1**

Pencil Materials . . . Things to Remember

1

Pencil Materials . . . Things to Remember

SKETCHING IS THE MOST INEXPENSIVE art medium. Nevertheless you will be well advised to splurge and get the best equipment on the market. It pays in the end. Although any old pencil and sheet of paper may be adequate, you can do better work with the materials professionals use. You can obtain this equipment at any reputable art store.

Pencils

The wider the selection of pencils you have, the more varied the effect you will achieve in your drawings. Here is a minimum basic list of pencils you should get:

Hard: 2H, H	Soft: 2B, 4B, 6B
Medium: HB	Very Soft: Layout pencil, Ebony pencil

Buy two or three of each pencil so you won't have  to keep running back to the store. There are many more pencils in the hard to soft range and I suggest you add new ones to your collection from time to  time—particularly layout pencils. These give rich, velvety blacks, and they are good for fast sketching.

Paper

Paper is most important. Without a good surface  to work on, even the best pencils will not produce the professional effect you want. The most practical paper for the beginner is a medium-surfaced  pencil pad. A pad keeps your sketches together and also makes a good foundation to work on. For general work, a practical size pad is 11 x 14 inches (18  x 36 cm). Pads come in various other standard sizes, like 6 x 8 (15 x 20 cm) and 8? x 11 (22 x 28  cm). Choose the sizes that suit you best. By all means include in your shopping list one or two pocket-size pads which you can carry with you  wherever you go on a plane, boat, bus, car or train. You never know when you will see a subject you want to sketch or make notes on. With a pad and a pencil in your pocket you will always be prepared.

Paper has a variety of surfaces: smooth, hard, soft, clay-coated, granular, etc. Some papers go by the trade names of Plate, Kid, Cameo, Bristol (smooth or soft). At first you may wonder which kind to use. Actually you can draw on any of them, but some papers are best for some pencils, others for others, and each combination will give a different effect.

On a smooth-surface paper you will find that fewer pencils are required, and these should tend to be soft ones. The rougher the paper surface, the harder the pencils you will need for gaining a smooth tone. For the average sketch, I recommend a smooth surface pad. Plate finish is good. For certain textural effects a rougher paper may be more suitable. In this case, experiment with the harder pencils. A rough paper is good when working with pencil and stump. See Project 4.

You may also want to experiment with sheets of paper not attached to a pad. There are many on the market and one of the best surfaces I have ever worked on has been a clay-coated surface produced for the printing industry.

Sometimes a very cheap paper, such as newsprint paper, is especially good when you're working with a very soft pencil. Newsprint paper comes in pads of various sizes and is very economical. I've even used tracing paper pads for sketching, and this paper also has a good surface for soft pencils. The best procedure is to get samples of many papers and experiment on them with different pencils until you discover the combination you like best. If you use single sheets, work on a smooth table or board and put a number of sheets under your working paper. These extra sheets make a good yielding surface, affecting the quality of pencil lines and tones. Nothing is more discouraging than drawing on a hard drawing board that does not have resiliency for your pencils.

Erasers

Kneaded eraser or dough eraser. You should use erasers as little as possible in pencil work; at times, however, they can be used purposely to obtain certain striking effects. The eraser can be a valuable tool if used judiciously.

Stump

Tortillon stump. This is a small paper tool which can produce a variety of effects if used cautiously. Its use is explained in Project 4.

Sandpaper Block

This is a very useful tool for beveling or sharpening the point of your lead. The sandblock with a handle is most convenient.

Tips on Sharpening

Most of us have used pencil sharpeners all our lives. For best results, forget this mechanical device and sharpen your pencils with a penknife or razor blade. With this method, knowing how much lead to expose for drawing and how thick to make the lead, you can get just the right point.

Keep the exposed lead of the pencil on the shorter side. Short leads do not break easily; therefore more pressure may be applied to the pencil to get strong lines and deep blacks.

A beveled point gives a broad stroke that is most effective for pencil brushing and sketching. For pure pencil sketching, especially the side-stroke technique, you may want to have a longer pointed lead on your pencil, since you do not need to apply as much pressure as with a beveled point.

PROJECT 2

Pencil Line

2
Pencil Line

A LINE DRAWING IS THE MOST DIRECT means of expression. This type of drawing, without shading or tone, is usually the first we attempt. A line drawing may be somewhat limited in effect, yet it conveys dimension, movement, structure and mood; it can also suggest texture to some extent.

Children are usually apt to convey their first impressions in line, and their lack of inhibitions and freedom of expression add great charm and character to their work. Modern artists too try to keep their forms simple and symbolic.

If you experiment with a few simple lines on a sheet of paper you will find that vertical lines, convey a sense of dignity; horizontal lines, repose; curved lines suggest grace and movement; zigzag lines, action. Thick and thin lines express third dimension as well as a sense of light and shade.

Child's drawing.   *Sketch by author.*

A line which is stiff and uniform in width is uninteresting; it lacks spark and zest. On the other hand, a sweeping line of varied width is full of vitality. Asian artists are great masters at line and employ it as a language rather than as a tool.

Let's start the project with a 2B pencil and some soft drawing paper. Sharpen the point of the pencil, preferably with a knife or razor blade, and bevel the point as indicated on page 16. This gives you the advantage of drawing a thick line as well as a thin line (with the sharp edge of the pencil) and may be employed as shown in the diagram. At first, don't try to sketch

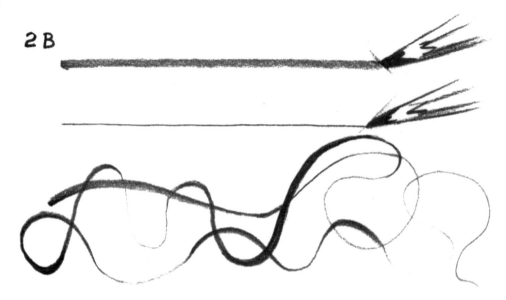

any specific object—just try out some practice lines. Make a few thick lines, then some thin ones on the same sheet of paper. Make some lines straight, others curved and sweeping. This practice will get you over your first tenseness. After doodling, you will feel more relaxed and in a mood to draw.

Now sharpen your pencil again, and on a fresh sheet of paper make a line drawing of an apple, grapes, or any other fruit. Or make a tree trunk and

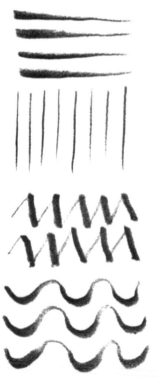

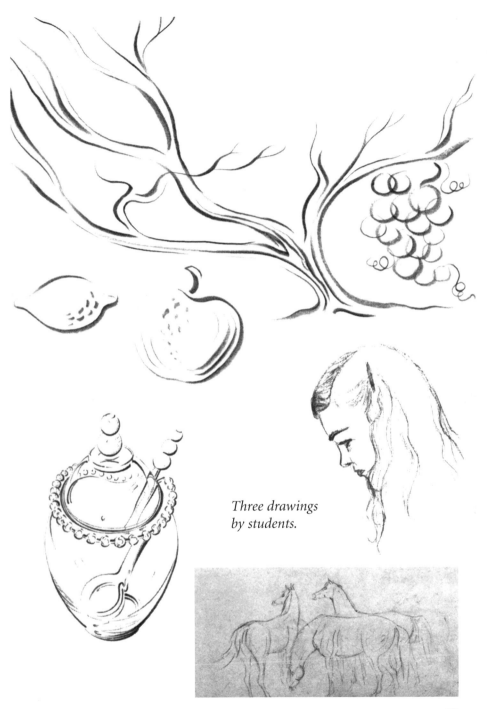

Three drawings by students.

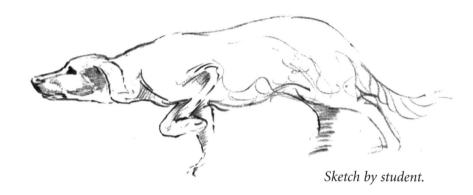

Sketch by student.

branches, employing thick and thin lines. Draw any simple object you like direct from nature. Study your subject well before you start. After making one drawing, set this aside and make another of the same object and yet a third. Don't copy what you did before, study your subject with new eyes each time. Later you can compare drawings and make another one incorporating the best features of the earlier ones if you want to. This will help you to see with the eyes of an artist. The more you draw the same subject, the more you learn about it and the different ways it can be interpreted even in a line drawing. Some examples of student work using the thick and thin line technique are shown on page 21.

Now try a pencil sharpened to a point instead of to a beveled edge. Select a grade HB pencil and sharpen. Note how easily one can draw with this point and how, if it is used in a side-stroke technique, it adds shading to your drawing. A few examples of pencil shading are given here. Line gives character, but shading gives depth and value—it is like adding an extra dimension to your sketch. So, as we go along, we will learn to employ both of these methods of drawing.

Sketch by author.

*Demonstration sketch by Ernest Watson for
the author's students at Pratt Institute.*

PROJECT 3

Pencil Painting

3
Pencil Painting

PENCIL PAINTING IS A TERM USED when we handle our pencil almost as if it were a brush. This method is intriguing. Your drawings will show a paintlike quality and a vigor and freshness not as easily attainable with other pencil techniques. Here value (tones from dark to light) rather than line, is the important factor. The amount of pressure you apply to the pencil will determine the value of your stroke. Darks are achieved with harder strokes, lighter values with a release of pressure.

Let's consider the question of texture. You will find that different textures are achieved on different kinds of paper. If the paper is rough, your texture will be granular and broken. If the paper is smooth your texture will be even, somewhat flat, but interesting nevertheless. Smooth papers are especially good for rendering glass, water, pottery, metal and for getting clear sharp results. Rough textures are good for rendering objects like wood and stone; they will give a lithographic quality to your work.

In brushing with your pencil, don't always run strokes evenly together; you will attain greater sparkle and more interesting texture if you allow some clear white paper to break through. This applies even to a quite solid area of tone.

In pencil painting, a number of different pencils may be employed—3B, 4B, or 6B, for instance. You can also use the wide flat lead of a layout or architect's pencil. Let's try a value scale using a number of pencils, as shown in the illustration below.

Now, do a drawing of a tree, preferably a gnarly old trunk with dead branches. If you can't find a suitable tree in your

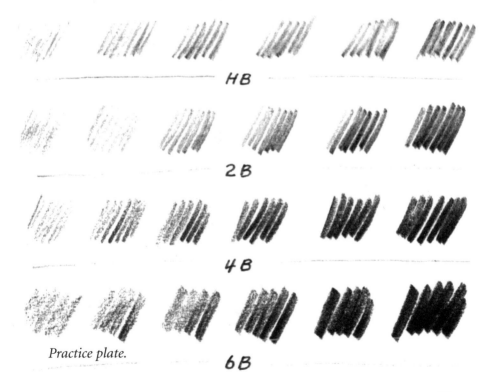

Practice plate.

neighborhood or you live in the city, find a good photograph of one in a magazine or book and work from that. It will make an interesting indoor project. But don't always do this, and don't always work indoors either. Outdoor sketching directly from nature is more stimulating. With the easy methods of transportation today, it takes only a short while to travel and work directly from nature. Carry a small sketching pad or some papers tacked to a small drawing board. Artists often sketch directly from nature, then later work up a finished drawing or painting indoors.

As you sketch, you will find that "tone values" are very important. The practice plate we just did was in a way a "tone

Student's work.

scale." It went from light to dark tones. The intensity of the tone establishes the key of the picture—for a high key we use the light

High key.   *Middle key.*   *Low key.*

tones; for the middle key, medium tones, and for the low key, dark tones. For a bright picture where intense light and shade are used, as on a bright sunny day, the whole tonal scale from light to dark may be employed. Usually, for general sketching,

Student's work.

Sketch by Ernest Watson.

the beginner will use the whole scale, but under special weather conditions, such as mist, fog, rain, night, moonlight, any one of the three tone keys might be used.

After pencil painting a few trees for practice, try a whole landscape and employ the full tonal scale. Choose any scene you like. You are the one who is going to draw, so select a subject that will give you the most pleasure. It may be a peaceful pastoral scene with cows grazing, or that New England barn you've always wanted to sketch; perhaps it will be a rocky coastline with jagged rocks and scrub oaks, or a city skyline with the bustle of cars and throngs of people. A little village nestled against a hillside fishing boats jauntily rocking in a salty harbor, a lighthouse, or the majestic mountains—these are a few other scenes which immediately come to mind.

Whatever you do, have an attitude of enjoyment toward your work. Sketching is not a prescription but a pleasure, and when you enjoy doing something, at once it becomes easier. Don't struggle with the pencil—have fun with it. If your first attempt seems feeble, don't be discouraged; take another sheet of paper and start again. Make quick sketches; make an overall impression of the scene; establish the main direction of lines and the areas of light and dark. Don't labor over details. You can practice details at home and incorporate them in another more finished sketch later if you want to.

Try to keep your drawing simple; learn to eliminate unnecessary detail and put in only what you deem to be essential—the skeleton of a scene, so to speak. Suggestion of detail is more interesting than a carefully finished study. In other words you don't have to draw every last blade of grass or its equivalent. Nine times out of ten, a rapid, free expression or impression of a scene is more alive than a meticulous, labored-over drawing.

Freshness is one of the keys to good sketching. Instead of erasing errors, get in the habit of making a fresh sketch. This will

Pencil painting by student.

Student's work.

better familiarize you with your subject; each sketch you do of the same theme or object is likely to be freer and more convincing than the last one.

After you have made a number of pencil paintings there may be some you want to keep and show your friends. Drawings smudge easily, but you can guard against this by spraying them with a fixative. This liquid comes in a spray bottle and can be obtained at any artists materials store. Spray the fixative on evenly from a distance. Don't use too much; spray a thin even coat.

Student's work.

Two-minute pencil painting by author.

PROJECT **4**

Pencil Tone and Stump

4
Pencil Tone and Stump

FROM INFANCY, PEOPLE have a desire to smear something, whether it be paint, grease, or mud. Tone and stump might be called the pencil equivalent of finger painting. However, while the fingers can occasionally be used to rub in a pencil tone, a simple paper tool called the "tortillon stump" is the approved tool. This little implement, obtainable at any artists materials store, is a tightly wound piece of paper tapered at one end. It is used to rub tones of pencil, carbon, crayons, or charcoal.

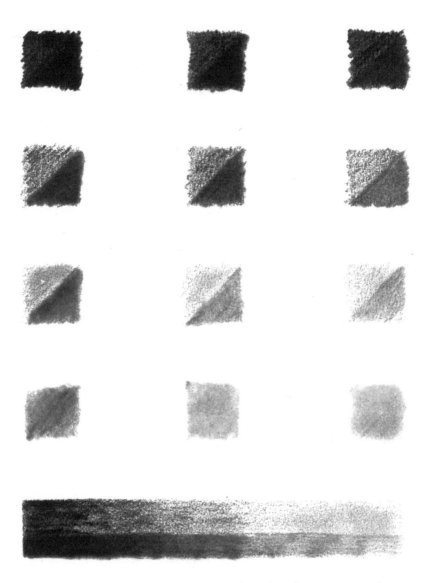

Practice plate: stump and tone.

Although a whole practice drawing might be done with a stump and a few sharp lines added for accent, the technique is usually reserved for details like shading. Tone and stump is most effective when handled judiciously. Its chief use is where a smooth tone effect is needed.

In order to build up enough graphite on the paper for the stump to work properly, a soft pencil like a 3B should be used. The best paper for tone and stump is a textured, rough paper. Here you may work in a larger area of pad or paper than before. With the soft lead pencil we "scumble" over the surface of the paper with rapid strokes, drawing rather freely and going back over the tones for darkening values.

After a quick drawing is made and the scumbling tones are put down, the tortillon stump comes into play and a little rubbing here and there is usually sufficient to give a pleasing, soft, textural effect. You will find that after some rubbing, the stump becomes blackened. If you wish, you may then use the stump as a brush and apply to parts that have not been penciled.

The practice plate (page 37) gives a good idea as to the value change when using the tortillon stump. Note how the value of the pencil tones can become darker and the texture smoother.

This medium is especially good for creating on paper the atmosphere of a soft pastoral scene, a foggy morning, a misty mountain. It may be effectively used for shadowing areas, for stone, trunks of trees, clouds, the fur of animals—wherever a

Student's drawing in stump and tone.

Stump and tone drawing by student.

Student's work.

very smooth or soft effect is desired. The examples on these pages show some of the subtle effects gained with the use of the stump.

Camille Corot. "Henry Leroy as a Child."

PROJECT **5**

Pencil Sketching

5
Pencil Sketching

T HE MOST ENJOYABLE AND PERHAPS the most care-
free of all the pencil techniques is "pencil sketching." The
very word "sketching" conjures up the thought of filling a
sketchbook full of quick impressions of
almost anything or of anyone who happens
to be around.

Get into the habit of carrying a sketch
pad with you, wherever you go. It is great
fun to be able to sketch this, that, and
everything at random. The more you do it,
the sooner you will gain experience. At the
same time, you will be developing a valuable
collection of information for any future
paintings or finished drawings you may want
to do in your home or studio.

Your sketches should be quick—
two to five minutes each. Draw rapidly to capture the action or atmosphere of the moment. Again, let me
stress, don't rework your sketches.
Turn the sheet over and start a new
one. Later you can decide which are
your best. I recall taking a sketch
pad with me to the circus one
year and enjoying two fascinating

hours of sketching my quick impressions. I set down
what I saw in the rings at a glance. This was necessary, for, as you
know, the circus changes every few minutes. It was good practice. For months afterward I enjoyed the circus by recalling each
act from these quick sketches. Then from the best studies, a

*Two- to five-minute drawings
from student's sketchbook.*

series of circus watercolors were made and exhibited later on. I also did several oil paintings based on these sketches.

By disciplining yourself to work fast you will eliminate that "worked over" look. Two-minute sketches preserve that feeling of spontaneity which is so necessary to a good drawing. Sketch anything that you happen to see at the moment—if you're on the beach with friends, don't be embarrassed sketching them; they'll have as much fun posing for you as you'll have drawing them. No one expects you to be a Michelangelo when you first start out.

Student's work.

Sketch scenes as you travel by train or bus—you will be surprised how a quick sketch can capture rolling hills, a road winding up a mountain, wheat fields and farm lands with barns and animals grazing. When traveling by car, stop for a few minutes at places that you would ordinarily photograph, and sketch the scene instead. It won't take much longer, and it will bring much more satisfaction.

Vacation time is always a good time for sketching. We are more relaxed when we are on holiday. If you don't travel or can't get away, there are always any number of scenes to sketch at home—the family, animals, birds, the garden, the old swimming hole, picnics, the view from your window whether in city or country, automobiles, trains—even interiors and your favorite objects in them are fun to do.

Although a teacher might ordinarily frown at a student copying from a photograph, I heartily endorse this procedure for occasional practice. As a temporary measure, and for new subject matter, a photograph can be useful study material, especially when time is limited to sketching in the evenings. Anything you can do to get practice with the pencil is useful. Always keep trying for new subjects and new ways of drawing them. Above all, have fun. If you vary your subject matter, drawing will never become dull.

As time goes on, think of organizing a group who will meet for sketching one evening a week, or take a picnic or cookout

Two rough sketches by author to be used as notes for finished drawings and paintings.

sketch trip on weekends. Members of a group can encourage one another and act as willing models. Such groups already exist in many communities. They are sponsored by adult education groups or private art programs.

To get back to our present project, let's use a soft 4B or 5B pencil on any paper you may choose—preferably a hard surface pad. Sharpen your pencil and make some practice strokes, holding the pencil between thumb and first finger with the pencil in the palm of your hand and the lead resting on the paper horizontally. You will find you can move rapidly over any given area in this side-stroke technique. The broad, rapid strokes cover a lot of ground quickly. By applying pressure on the pencil, you will attain rich

Student's sketch.

Samuel Chamberlain. "St. Clement Danes."

black tones. Or by skimming lightly over the surface with your pencil, you will attain a delicate tone. Note as you practice this technique that the pencil not only moves easily in any desired direction, but that you can change your direction with very little effort. You will find that a soft pencil has a tendency to break easily, especially if the lead is too long. Always keep your

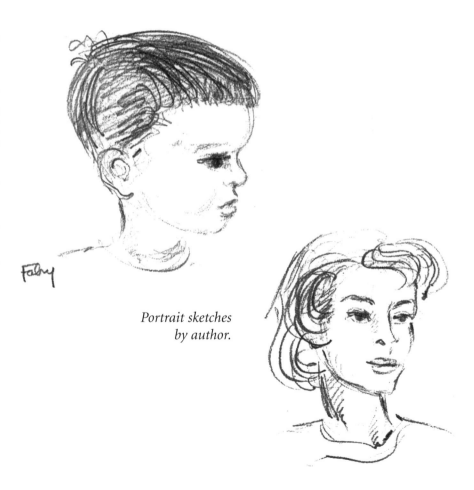

*Portrait sketches
by author.*

Marcel Vertes. Drawing.

pencil sharp, and cut the lead to a shorter length if it breaks too readily. Leave more wood on the topside to strengthen the lead. If need be, hold your finger on the lead itself, especially when applying more pressure to your rendering.

You will find that the side of the pencil will give nice, wide strokes for broad areas. For detail, assume a normal writing position with the pencil. After trying out the pencil in many different ways to get the feel of it, take a new piece of paper and make a quick two minute sketch of any object that interests you, then another and another. Then take a rest. Don't get tired.

You will note that I have suggested the use of only one pencil. This is because when sketching rapidly, it is difficult to change from one pencil to another and still maintain a spontaneous pace and rhythm. Pencil is a most expressive medium and a few lines can very often express more than a detailed rendering. Sketch to your heart's content—sketch boats, figures, trees, flowers, architecture, friends, animals, city life, country scenes, beach scenes, an apple, a book, a chair, your kitchen utensils. Recollect some of your childhood days, the schoolhouse, ice skating, the bus or trolley cars. Select any subject that will give you a personal interest. Never allow yourself to get discouraged. Rest between times—then sketch again. Get the outline and the movement of your subject down in bold strokes; fill in any details you want to later.

The drawings included here should encourage you and show a few different styles of pencil sketching.

Eduard Manet. "The Racetrack."

Other Pencil Variations

6

Other Pencil Variations

LASTLY, WE SHOULD KNOW ABOUT wash and benzine. The following variations are not an essential part of a beginner's training, but they will add a little diversion to your studies. You will very likely want to return to these techniques and develop them later on.

Pencil and Wash

After you have first made a light preliminary drawing of your subject in line only, try applying a wash over the drawing as though you were doing a watercolor. You may use ivory black, sepia, or neutral gray (black mixed with white) watercolor in conjunction with the pencil. The use of these harmonizing monochromatic colors does not detract from the color or quality of the pencil.

Demonstration pencil and wash drawing. The four values shown on the facing page are all that are needed for a basic wash rendering.

Your drawing remains basically a pencil rendering with the addition of wash for a pleasing variety of tone and texture.

Mix your color with water on a palette and apply the wash lightly. Cover your large areas, principally in the dark shadow and halftone areas. Keep the wash light in value, using plenty of water, so that it does not overshadow the pencil. Then when the wash has thoroughly dried, go back over the areas which you wish to accentuate and darken them with pencil.

The combination of pencil and wash makes a pleasing effect, as shown in the examples on these pages. Do a few practice washes, as indicated at left, in varying values. Note what richness the pencil over the wash adds to your drawing.

Student's pencil and wash drawing.

Pencil and Benzine

Using benzine will make you feel rather like the cat that swallowed the canary. You will feel as smug and self-satisfied as he, when you have worked with this medium. Here we start with the pencil drawing first, using a soft pencil. Then we take a sable-haired watercolor brush and dip it into the benzine, and wash over the pencil areas. This is different from the wash technique in that the benzine does not in itself add color; it merely modifies the shaded pencil areas. The benzine solution immediately dissolves the graphite and gives a soft wash effect in the lighter

Practice plate. Pencil with benzine.

pencil areas and a black, inky tone in the dark ones. it is a highly effective technique, but the danger lies in smearing too much of this solution over your whole drawing. Therefore, use the benzine very sparingly. Soft fuzzy objects like the kitten shown here may be rendered to advantage by this unusual method. Besides animals, try subjects like trees, shrubs, and flowers.

In all types of drawing a sense of good design and individuality are most desirable. Use good taste and keep experimenting with new effects and techniques. Sketching with pencil is fun—every stroke of the way.

Student's pencil and benzine drawing.

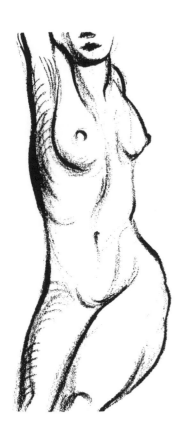

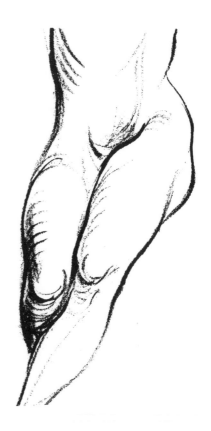

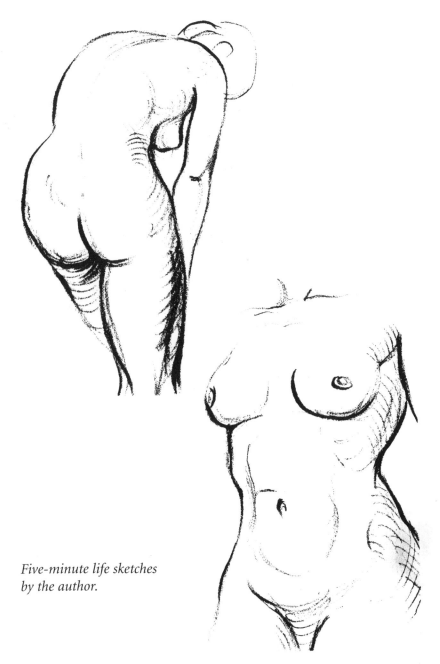

Five-minute life sketches by the author.

Honoré Daumier. "Two Judges."